Quilt Block Party

Series #1 - Quilter's Year
© 1988 by Eleanor Burns

Quilt in a Day®

1955 Diamond Street
San Marcos, CA 92069

Table of Contents

Make a new block every month and set the twelve blocks together in a monthly chronological order. All blocks can be constructed in one hour or less with easy assembly sewing methods. Nine blocks are made from strips, squares, and rectangles, while three blocks are cut from template patterns provided.

Approximate Finished Size: 48" x 63"

Twelve 12" Blocks

Yardage

Choose two main colors, and purchase a light, medium, and dark of each. Use this yardage when making the twelve blocks throughout the year.

In addition, mix the scales of your prints. Choose a large scale print, a small scale print, and a solid, or one that looks like a solid from a distance in each main color.

When choosing your fabrics for each new block during the year, select fabrics different from those in the adjacent completed blocks.

First Main Color

3/4 yd. first light

3/4 yd. first medium

3/4 yd. first dark

Second Main Color

3/4 yd. second light

3/4 yd. second medium

3/4 yd. second dark

In Addition, Purchase

1/2 yd. muslin

Bonded Batting

Pieces for Machine Quilting

If you wish to machine quilt the individual block following each Block Party, purchase lightweight batting at the first Party.

2 1/2 yds. of 48" wide batting or 1 3/4 yds. of 96" wide batting

Cut into twelve pieces

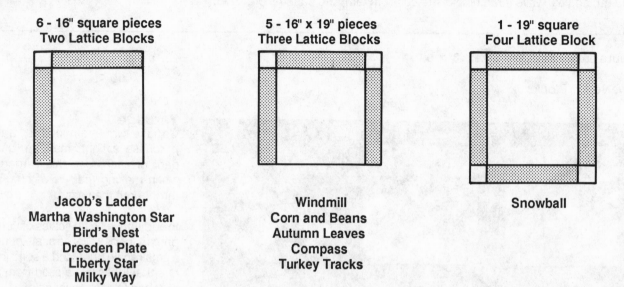

6 - 16" square pieces
Two Lattice Blocks

Jacob's Ladder
Martha Washington Star
Bird's Nest
Dresden Plate
Liberty Star
Milky Way

5 - 16" x 19" pieces
Three Lattice Blocks

Windmill
Corn and Beans
Autumn Leaves
Compass
Turkey Tracks

1 - 19" square
Four Lattice Block

Snowball

One Large Piece of Batting

If you do not wish to machine quilt each individual block, but finish with a "quick turn" once all the unquilted blocks are sewn together, do not purchase the batting until the last block is completed. Select a thick batting that shows dimension when the layers are tied together.

1 7/8 yds. of 48" wide batting

Lattice and Backing

Purchase a solid color of 100% cotton that coordinates with your two main colors.

Lattice: 1 1/4 yds.
Cut (11) strips 3 1/2" wide by 45" long.
Cut the long strips into (31) 3 1/2" x 12 1/2" strips.

Backing: 3 yds.
Cut into two equal pieces and seam together lengthwise.

Cornerstones

Purchase a 100% cotton nondirectional calico print that coordinates with your two main colors and your solid colored lattice.

Cornerstones: 1/4 yd.
Cut into (20) 3 1/2" squares.

Supplies Needed

Rotary cutter, gridded cutting mat, 6" x 24" ruler with a 45° line, 12 1/2" Square Up, 6" square ruler, marking pencil, magnetic seam guide, neutral thread, polyester spun invisible thread, scissors, template paper or plastic , floss 1 yard thin cording.

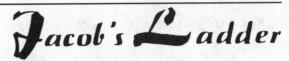

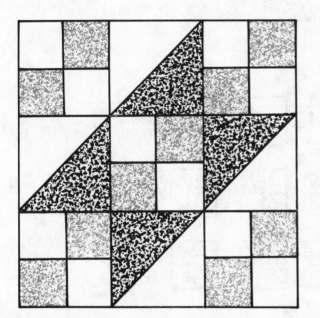

Biblical Jacob, fearing death because he tricked both his father and brother, fled from home. One evening as he slept with his head resting on a stone for a pillow, he dreamt of angels of God ascending and descending on a ladder stretching from heaven to earth. The women of Colonial America used the light and darks to show the brilliant staircase sparkling in the night sky.

Likewise, the same pattern could look like a kite with flapping tails soaring in the wind, and thus was also known as the Tail of Benjamin's Kite in eastern United States.

President Dwight D. Eisenhower and his brother cut up the scraps for the Jacob's Ladder quilt on display at his birthplace in Denison, Texas.

Others referred to the pattern as Underground Railroad, Trail of Covered Wagons, Wagon Tracks, Road to California, and Rocky Road to Oklahoma.

Choose a light, medium, and dark for Jacob's Ladder.

Cutting Instructions

Layer Cut with Right Sides Together:

(1) 2 5/8" x 30" light
(1) 2 5/8" x 30" medium

(1) 5" x 10" light
(1) 5" x 10" dark

Use an accurate 1/4" seam allowance and 15 stitches per inch.

Sewing the Five

1. Seam the 2 5/8" strips together lengthwise.

2. Press the seam to the medium side.

3. Cut into (10) 2 5/8" sections.

4. Place 5 in each stack in this order:

Flip the piece on the right to the piece on the left. Match the center seam. Stitch. Butt the second set behind the first set and continue. Assembly line sew all sets in this manner.

Sewing the Four

1. Draw on a 5" grid. Draw on diagonal lines.

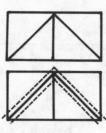

2. Sew a 1/4" seam on both sides of the diagonal lines.

3. Cut apart on all lines. Press the seams to the dark side.

4. Trim off the tips.

Sewing the Block Together

1. Lay the pieces out in this order:
   Flip the second vertical row right sides together
   to the first vertical row.

2. Continuously sew together the vertical row.
3. Flip the third vertical row to the second vertical row.
   Continuously sew.
   Do not snip the threads holding the rows together.

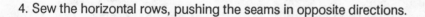

4. Sew the horizontal rows, pushing the seams in opposite directions.

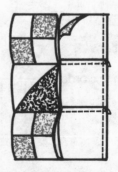

Jacob's Ladder is the top left corner block of the quilt.

(Optional) Machine Quilting Jacob's Ladder to a Two Lattice Piece of Batting

1. Place the block in the lower right hand corner of the 16" square piece of lightweight bonded batting. Pin in place.
2. Thread your sewing machine with the lightweight polyester spun invisible thread. Loosen your top tension, and lengthen your stitch to 8-10 stitches per inch.
3. Load your bobbin with neutral sewing thread.
4. Place the needle in the depth of the seam by the dot, and "stitch in the ditch" around the dark triangles following the arrows. Stitch continuously without removing the block from the machine, pivoting with the needle in the fabric at the points.

5. Pin a 3 1/2" x 12 1/2" lattice strip right sides together to the left side of the block. Stitch through all thicknesses. Fold back.

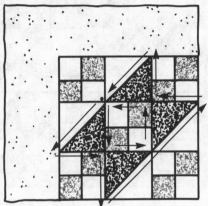

6. Sew a 3 1/2" cornerstone to one lattice strip.

7. Pin it right sides together to the top of the block. Stitch. Fold back flat.

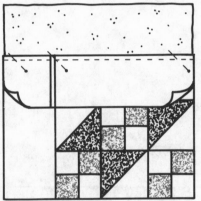

Other Two Lattice Blocks

In the same manner as described, five other blocks will be sewn to a 16" square piece of bonded batting and two lattice strips added.

FEBRUARY

Martha Washington Star

APRIL

Bird's Nest

MAY

Dresden Plate

JULY

Liberty Star

AUGUST

Milky Way

Jacob's Ladder Quilt
18 Blocks (3 x 6)
36" x 72"

Jacob's Ladder Quilt
24 Blocks (4 x 6)
48" x 72"

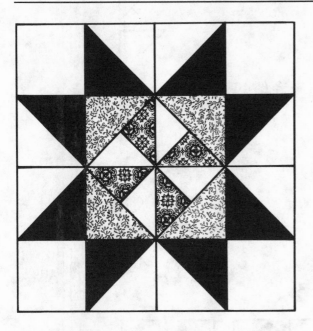

Martha Washington's Star

For many years quilters have paid special tribute to women they truly admired by creating a quilt block in their name. History not only honors Martha Washington for her style and strength of character, but also credits her as being an appreciator of quilting. In the records of sales of the Fairfax estate at Belvoir, Virginia, there is included the item, "George Washington purchased 19 coverlets or quilts to take back home to Martha at Mt. Vernon."

Choose one light, one medium, and two darks.

Cutting Instructions

Star
Layer cut right sides together:
(1) 4" x 16" light
(1) 4" x 16" first dark

Frame Around Pinwheel
(2) 4" squares medium
Cut in halves on diagonal

Center Pinwheel
(1) 4 1/2" square second dark
(1) 4 1/2" square light
Cut in fourths on the diagonals

Corners
(4) 3 5/8" squares light

Use an accurate 1/4" seam allowance and 15 stitches per inch.

Making the Star

1. Place the 4" x 16" light and first dark rectangles right sides together.

2. Draw on 4" square lines.
   Draw on diagonal lines. Pin together.

3. Sew 1/4" seams on both sides of the diagonal lines. Begin sewing at the X.

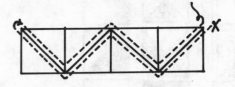

4. Cut apart on all lines.
5. Press the seams to the dark side.
6. Trim off the tips.

Making the Pinwheel

1. Place the 4 1/2" second dark and light squares cut into fourths in this order:

2. Assembly line sew them together.

3. Press the seams to the dark side.

Making the Center

1. Place the pinwheel and 4" medium square cut on the diagonal in this order:

2. Assembly line sew.

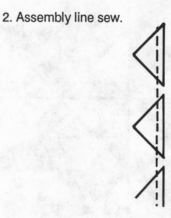

3. Press the seams to the medium side.

4. Trim off the tips.

Sewing the Block Together.

1. Lay all the pieces out in this order:

2. Sew all vertical rows.

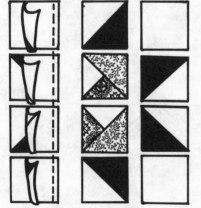

3. Sew the horizontal rows.

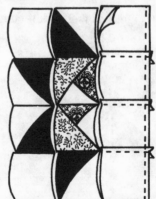

Martha Washington Star is the center block in the top row of the quilt.

(Optional) Machine Quilting a Two Lattice Block

1. Pin the block to the corner of a 16" square piece of bonded batting. Continuously "stitch in the ditch" around the star and pinwheel.

2. Add the lattice and cornerstone. *See Jacob's Ladder for more detail.*

8

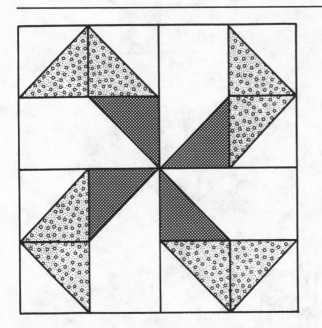

Windmill

It's no small wonder that women designed a quilt block to commemorate the windmill. Not only was the common water pumper depended upon in rural areas to irrigate farmland, but it was also used for milling grain, sawing wood, making paper, pressing oil from seeds, and grinding many different materials.

Choose a light, medium, and dark.

Cutting Instructions

Layer Cut Right Sides Together
(1) 8" square light
(1) 8" square medium

(2) 4" squares dark

(4) 3 1/2" x 6 1/2" rectangles light

Use an accurate 1/4" seam allowance and 15 stitches per inch.

Making the

1. With the 8" squares of light and medium right sides together, draw a 4" grid on the light.

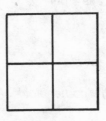

2. Draw on diagonal lines. Pin.

3. Sew a 1/4" seam on both sides of the diagonal lines.

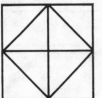

4. Cut apart on all lines.

5. Press the seams to the medium side.

6. Arrange them in two stacks of four each in this order: Assembly line sew them together.

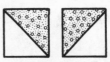

7. Press the seams to one side. Clip the threads holding them together.

Making the

1. Cut the two 4" squares of dark in half on the diagonal.

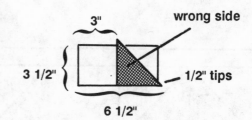

2. Place the dark triangles right sides together to the 3 1/2" x 6 1/2" rectangles of light in this order: Pin.

3. Assembly line sew.

4. Press the dark triangle over and flat onto the rectangle. Trim away the bottom part of the rectangle.

Making the

1. Lay the two stacks of four each in this order:
2. Assembly line sew them together.

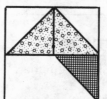
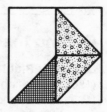

Sewing the Block Together

1. Rearrange them in this order:

2. Sew the vertical rows.

3. Sew the horizontal rows.

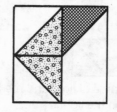
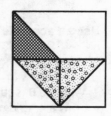

Windmill is the top right corner block of the quilt.

(Optional) Machine Quilting a Three Lattice Block

1. Pin the block in the bottom center of a 16" x 19" piece of bonded batting.

2. Beginning in the center, "stitch in the ditch" on each half of the windmill following the directional arrows.

3. Add a lattice strip to the left side of the block through all thicknesses.

4. Add cornerstones to two lattice strips. Sew them to the block.

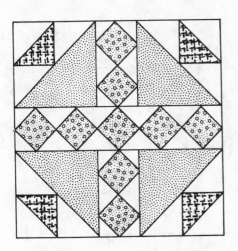

BIRD'S NEST

Quilters of the past paid special attention to the first signs of Spring as they kept watch over their gardens. The Bird's Nest Quilt Block was created in celebration of motherhood and symbolizes the strength of the home and family.

Choose a light, a first medium for the center squares (Eggs), a second medium for the large triangles (Nest), and a dark (Bird).

Cutting Instructions

Layer Cut Right Sides Together

(1) 3 1/2" x 7" light
(1) 3 1/2" x 7" dark (Bird)

(2) 2 1/4" x 45" strips light
(1) 2 1/4" x 45" strips first medium (Eggs)

Cut On the Diagonal

(2) 6" squares second medium (Nest)
(4) 3 1/2" squares light

Use an accurate 1/4" seam allowance and 15 stitches per inch.

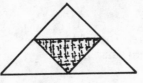

Making the Bird and the Corner

1. With the 3 1/2" x 7" pieces of light and dark right sides together, draw on 3 1/2" square lines.
2. Draw on diagonal lines.

3. Sew 1/4" seam on both sides of the diagonal line.
4. Cut on all lines.

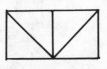

5. Press the seams to the dark side.

6. Place in this order with 4 triangles cut from the 3 1/2" squares of light:

Flip right sides together, matching the top edge. Let the tip hang over at the bottom. Assembly line sew. Press. Cut apart.

7. Lay this piece with the remaining 4 triangles in this order:

Match the bottom squares. Let the tips hang over at the top. Assembly line sew. Press. Cut apart.

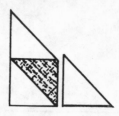

Adding the Nest to the Bird and Corner

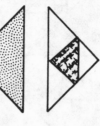

1. Lay the Bird with the second medium triangles in this order:

Flip right sides together. Assembly line sew, being careful not to cut off the points on the birds. Press. Cut apart.

Making the Eggs

1. Sew the 2 1/4" strips of light and first medium right sides together.

2. Press the seams to the middle.

3. Cut into (13) 2 1/4" sections. Divide them into two separate piles.

4. Place them so that the second piece is one step lower than the previous piece.

5. Flip the second piece right sides together to the first. The light on the top piece should extend up over the medium seam by 1/4". Match and fingerpin the seam. Stitch to the end.

6. Butt on and stitch all pairs. Clip apart.

7. Sew all pairs together into one long piece.

8. Trim off the "tips" of the strip 3/8" from the edge of the eggs.

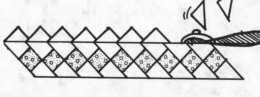

9. Cut 2 segments to include two eggs; they should measure approximately 2 3/4" x 5 1/2".

10. Cut 1 segment to include five eggs; it should measure approximately 2 3/4" x 12 1/2".

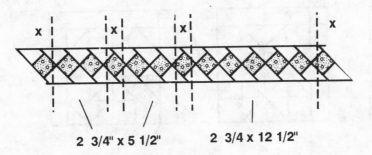

2 3/4" x 5 1/2"   2 3/4 x 12 1/2"

The Xed parts are eliminated.

Sewing the Block Together

1. Lay them out in this order:

2. Sew the top and bottom rows together. Stretch or ease to meet.

3. Pin and sew in the middle row, carefully matching the center.

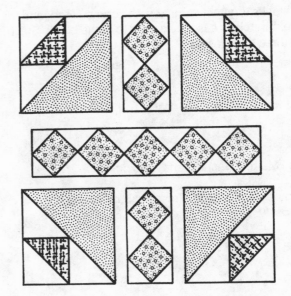

4. Square up to 12 1/2".

Bird's Nest is the first block in the second row of the quilt.

(Optional) Machine Quilting a Two Lattice Block
1. Pin the block to the corner of a 16" square piece of bonded batting.
2. "Stitch in the ditch" around the second medium triangles or nest, and the eggs.
3. Add the lattice and cornerstone. *See Jacob's Ladder for more detail.*

13

(Optional) Sewing the Machine Quilted Blocks into the First Row

The first three blocks, Jacob's Ladder, Martha Washington Star, and Windmill, are now ready to sew into the first row.

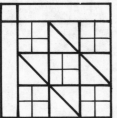 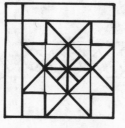 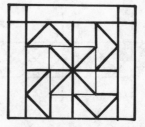

1. Lay the blocks out in monthly chronological order.

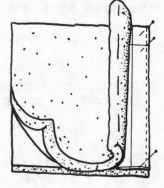

2. Flip Martha Washington Star right sides together to Jacob's Ladder. Snip the batting 1/2" away from the seam at the cornerstone. Fold back the top batting so you have only three layers to sew through: the batting on the bottom, the block, and the border.

3. Pin the two blocks together at the top, the cornerstone, and the bottom edge. Stretch or ease the border to fit the block. Stitch through the three thicknesses.

4. Fold back the Martha Washington Star block.

5. Trim away any excess batting. Press the batting into place and whipstitch loosely.

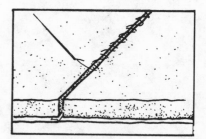

6. Flip Windmill right sides together to Martha Washington Star.

7. Snip the top batting from the cornerstone seam, fold back the batting, and pin.

8. Stretch or ease the border to fit the block. Stitch through the three thicknesses. Hand whipstitch the folded back batting in place.

All four rows are sewn from left to right in this manner.

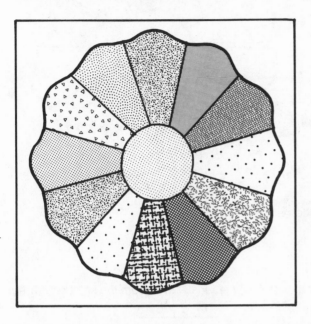

Dresden Plate

The Dresden Plate quilt name is based on a popular china made in Dresden, Germany between the early 1700's and the late 1800's. This delicate porcelain was decorated in a variety of bright colors and gold.

The quilt pattern is a combination of both piecing and applique. In its original form, each of the petals in the plate had a curved outer edge. As it passed from one quiltmaker to another it underwent changes so that frequently it is seen with pointed rather than rounded edges. It can be a delightful scrap quilt! The center is usually done in a solid color fabric which may or may not also appear in the wedges.

Choose a light background and an assortment of twelve different fabrics. Fabrics may be used more than once.

Cutting Instructions

Layer Cut:
(12) wedges from fabric assortment
(2) 4" squares of one fabric for center circle

(1) 12 1/2" sq. light or muslin background
(1) 11" sq. muslin lining

Use an accurate 1/4" seam allowance and 15 stitches per inch.

Sewing the 12 Wedges Together into the Plate

1. Assembly line sew the 12 wedges from the wide to the narrow into pairs.

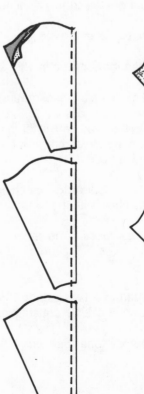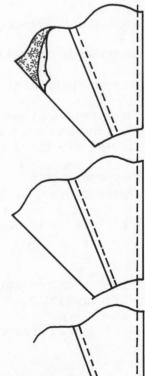

2. Sew the pairs into fourths, the fourths into halves, and then the halves into one whole circle.

3. Carefully press the seams in the circle to one side. Do not
   stretch out the circle.

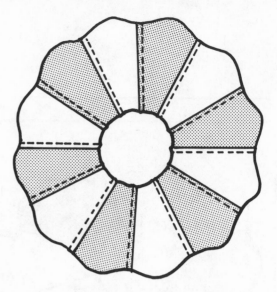

4. Place the Dresden circle right sides together to the 11" sq of
   muslin lining. Pin well around the bias edges.

5. Stitch around the outside edge, pivoting with the needle in
   the seam at the "corners."

6. Trim away the muslin and dresden edge to 1/16". Clip the "corners."

7. Turn right side out through the center opening. Work the edges gently until
   they are rounded.

8. Press so that the muslin does not show on the right side. *(Optional: Trim the muslin to 1" from the stitched edge.)*

Making the Center Circle

1. Trace the center circle onto the (2) 4" squares right sides together. Pin.

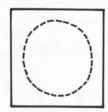

2. Sew on the line around the circle.

3. Trim and clip to 1/16" from the edge. Clip a hole in the back only. Turn right side out through the hole.

4. Press so that only the top layer is exposed.

Sewing the Plate to the Light or Muslin 12 1/2" Background Square

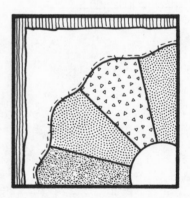

1. Center the plate and circle on the background. Pin.

2. Set your machine with the blind hem stitch on 1 1/2 stitch width.
   Use invisible thread on the top and regular thread in the bobbin.
   Loosen the top thread tension.

3. Sew closely around the outside edge, catching the edge of the
   Dresden plate and the circle with the blind hem.

Dresden Plate is the center block in the second row of the quilt.

(Optional) Machine Quilting a Two Lattice Block
1. Pin the block to the corner of a 16" square piece of bonded batting. Stitch 1/4" from the outside edge of
   the Dresden plate.
2. Add the lattice and cornerstone. *See Jacob's Ladder for more detail.*

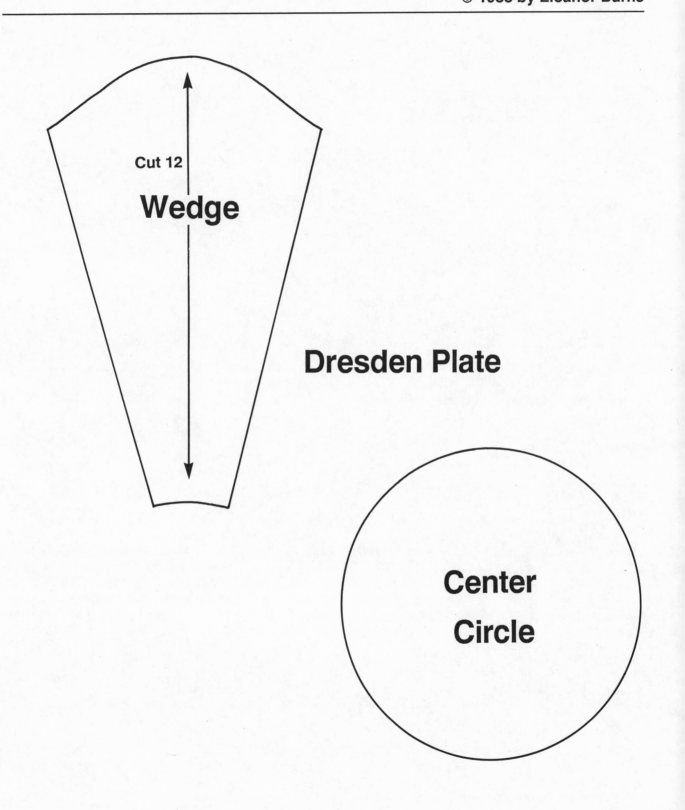

Cut 12

Wedge

Dresden Plate

Center Circle

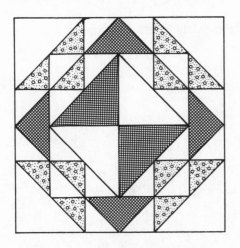

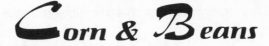

Perhaps it was corn and bean time of year when this lovely old pattern was first made into a quilt. It may have taken its homely name from the golden corn color with green and un-bleached muslin which formed its color scheme. The block is also known as Hen and Chickens, Shoofly, and Handy Andy.

Choose a light, medium, and dark for Corn and Beans.

Cutting Instructions

Layer Cut With Right Sides Together:

(1) 6" x 6" light
(1) 6" x 6" dark

(1) 3" x 6" light
(1) 3" x 6" medium

Cut On the Diagonal:

(1) 5" square light
(1) 5" square dark
(2) 5 1/8" squares light
(4) 3" squares light
(4) 3" squares medium

Use a full and accurate 1/4" seam allowance and 15 stitches per inch.

Making the

1. With the 3" x 6" pieces of light and medium right sides together, draw on 3" square lines.

2. Draw on diagonal lines.

3. Sew a 1/4" seam on both sides of the diagonal line.

4. Cut apart on all lines.

5. Press the seams to the dark side. Cut off the tips.

6. Place in this order with 4 triangles cut from the light 3" squares.

7. Flip right sides together, matching the top edge. Let the tip hang over at the bottom. Assembly line sew. Press. Cut apart.

8. Lay this piece with the remaining 4 light triangles in this order:
9. Match the bottom squares. Let the tips hang over at the top. Assembly line sew. Press. Cut apart.

Adding The Large Triangles

1. Lay two dark triangles and two light triangles cut from the 5" squares in this order:

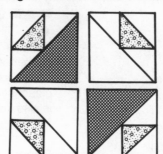

2. Flip right sides together. Assembly line sew, being careful not to cut off the points. Press. Cut apart.

3. Lay out the four center pieces of the block.

4. Sew together. Set aside.

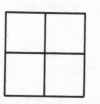

Making the Four

1. With the 6" square pieces of light and dark right sides together, draw on 3" lines.

2. Draw on diagonal lines, sew a 1/4" from the diagonal line, cut apart, and press the seams to the dark side. Cut off the tips.

3. Arrange them in two stacks of four each in this order:

4. Assembly line sew them together. Press. Clip the threads. Cut off the tips.

5. With two stacks of 4 medium triangles each, arrange and assembly line sew them in this order:

First Step

Second Step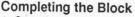

Completing the Block

1. Sew the four sections to the center in clockwise order, folding out each section after it is sewn. Allow tips to hang over at each end. Match the seams.
2. Sew the four light triangles cut from the 5 1/8" squares to the corners in the same clockwise order, allowing tips to hang over equally on both ends.
3. Square up to as close to 12 1/2" as you can get without trimming off the 1/4" seam allowance.

Corn and Beans is the last block of the second row in the quilt.

(Optional) Machine Quilting a Three Lattice Block
1. Pin the block in the bottom center of a 16" x 19" piece of bonded batting.
2. "Stitch in the ditch" around the dark triangles.
3. Add lattice and cornerstones. *See Windmill for more detail.*

(Sew the Second Horizontal row together.) *See Bird's Nest for more detail.*

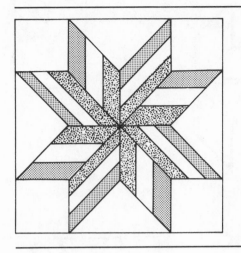

LIBERTY STAR

Recognizing the Liberty Star quilt block is an especially appropriate way of celebrating our country's independence. Even in years gone by, Liberty Star quilts were often given to young men as they became of age to join the service. You can just feel the pride and strength in a gift with such patriotism. And you can also imagine the comfort and security which a Liberty Star Quilt must have provided for anxious families as they waited for their sons to return safely home.

Choose a light, medium, and dark.

Cutting Instructions

(1) 1 3/8" x 45" light
(1) 1 3/8" x 45" medium
(1) 1 3/8" x 45" dark

(4) 4 3/8" squares light
(1) 6 5/8" square light

Use an accurate 1/4" seam allowance and 15 stitches per inch.

Use 6" x 12" or 6" x 24" ruler with a 45° line.

Making the Star
1. Seam the three strips together lengthwise with the light in the middle.
2. Press the seams to the dark and medium sides.
(The sewn together strip should measure 3". Sliver trim if necessary.)
3. Square off the left end. Discard.

4. Line up the 45° line on the squared off end. Trim. Discard.

5. Line up the 45° line on the top edge of the strip. Line up the diagonal cut with the 3" line. Cut. Continue to cut a total of eight diamonds in this manner.

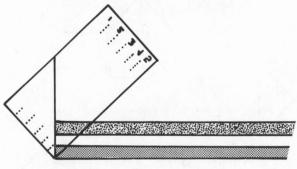

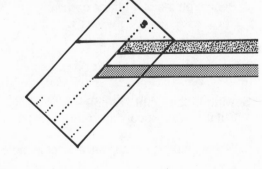

6. Divide the eight diamonds into two equal piles.

7. Flip the diamond on the right onto the diamond on the left. Sew the diamonds together from the center point out to 1/4" from the edge. Do not backstitch. Sew all diamonds together.

8. Press. Square off the pairs of diamonds using the end of the ruler.

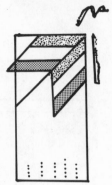

9. Lay out the star design.

10. Flip the right half of the star onto the left half of the star.

11. Stitch down the center and across, matching the center, and beginning and ending 1/4" from the end.

12. Flip the star and stitch, pushing the seams in opposite directions at the center.

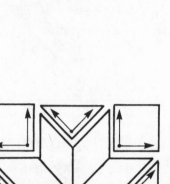

When sewing the light corners and light triangles onto the star follow the direction of the arrows as shown.

Sewing in the Light Corners

1. With a marking pencil, place a dot 1/4" in on one corner of each square.

2. At one corner of the star, right sides together, pin the 1/4" open seam of the diamond with the dot on the square.

3. Stitch to the outside edge.
4. Swing the square to meet the diamond edge and sew from the dot to the point.
5. Repeat on the other three corners.

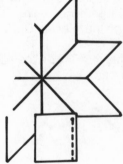

Sewing in the Light Triangles
1. Cut the 6 5/8" square into fourths on the diagonals.

2. With a marking pencil, place a dot in the corner of the triangle 1/4" in from the outside edge.

3. Working on one side at a time, sew the triangles into the middle of the sides, stitching from the 1/4" dot to the outside edges.
4. Square the block to 12 1/2".

Liberty Star is the first block in the third row.

(Optional) Machine quilt Liberty Star as a Two Lattice Block. *See Jacob's Ladder for more detail.*

MILKY WAY

The Milky Way, a bright band of light in the night sky from over 100 billion stars, inspired the quilter to desgin a block with swirling light and dark stars. While viewing the Milky Way on a clear moonless night this August, also watch for a spectacular show of "shooting" or "falling" stars. Actually, the stars are small pieces of rocky or metallic debris flying into the earth's atmosphere from outer space at such a great speed that the friction with the air causes them to glow!

Choose a light, medium, and dark.

Cutting Instructions

Layer Cut Right Sides Together

(2) 3" squares light
(2) 3" squares medium

(1) 1 3/4" x 36" strip light
(1) 1 3/4" x 36" strip dark

(1) 7" x 10 1/2" light
(1) 7" x 10 1/2" medium

Use an accurate 1/4" seam allowance and 15 stitches per inch.

Making the Nine

1. Sew the 1 3/4" strips of light and dark together lengthwise.

2. Press the seam to the dark side.

3. Cut into (18) 1 3/4" sections.

4. Make two stacks with nine in each.

5. Assembly line sew them together in this order:

6. Press open. Cut apart. Approximate size: 3" square

Making the Twelve

1. Place the 7" x 10 1/2" pieces of light and medium right sides together on the gridded board.

2. Draw on 3 1/2" square lines.

3. Draw on diagonal lines every other row beginning in the marked corner.

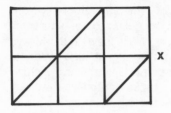

4. Draw on diagonal lines in the remaining rows in the opposite direction.

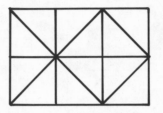

5. Flip the piece around and starting at the x, sew a 1/4" seam on both sides of the diagonal lines.

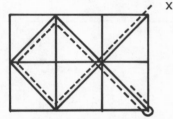 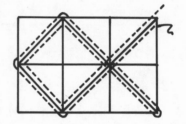

6. Cut apart on the 3 1/2" square lines and diagonal lines.

7. Press the seams to the dark side. Trim off the tips. Approximate Size: 3" Square

Sewing the Block Together

1. Lay all pieces out in this order:

2. Sew the vertical rows.

3. Sew the horizontal rows.

4. Square up to 12 1/2".

Milky Way is the second block in the third row in the quilt.

(Optional) Machine Quilting a Two Lattice Block
1. Pin the block to the corner of a 16" square piece of bonded batting.
2. "Stitch in the ditch" around the dark stars.
3. Add the lattice and cornerstone. *See Jacob's Ladder for more information.*

Making the Milky Way Quilt

This block as illustrated for the Quilt Block Party is comprised of 25 pieces. When making a quilt of Milky Way Blocks, all 25 pieces are not used in each block.

First Row of Quilt: The first block in the row is made with all twenty-five pieces. However, each block after the first one has the first vertical row eliminated and is made of only 20 pieces.

Second Row of Quilt: The first block in the second row is made with the top horizontal row eliminated and is made of only 20 pieces. Each block after the first block has both the top horizontal row and the first vertical row eliminated and is made of only 16 pieces.

Remaining Rows are made the same as the second row.

First Row

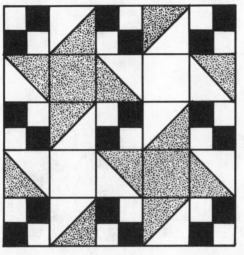

25 pieces

20 pieces

Second Row

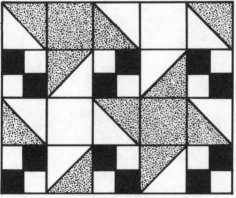

20 pieces

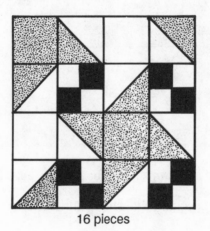

16 pieces

Milky Way Baby Quilt

Approximate finished size: 38" x 48" including 2" borders

First Row: (1) 25 piece block, (2) 20 piece blocks

Second, Third, and Fourth Rows: (1) 20 piece block, (2) 16 piece blocks

Autumn Leaves

New England Quilters of colonial times spent many a crisp fall morning outdoors, collecting brilliantly colored leaves and pressing them in a favorite book for safe keeping. It was only natural for them to bring the beauty of autumn leaves into their homes along with splendid rich cotton fabrics, billowy warm cotton batting, and this month's quilt block, Autumn Leaves.

Choose four different mediums or darks for the leaves, one light background color, and one medium or dark color for the center of the square.

Cutting Instructions

Layer Cut From Each of the Four Leaves:

(1) 2 3/4" x 5 1/2" (Points)
(1) 2 3/8" x 4 1/8"
(1) 2 3/8" square
(1) 1 1/2" x 4" strip cut on the bias (Stems)

Cut bias by lining up the 45° line on the ruler with the straight edge of the fabric. Cut on the angle and discard. Measure and cut a 1 1/2" strip on that angle.

Center of the Square

(1) 2 3/8" square

Cut from the Light Background

(1) 2 3/4" x 22"
(2) 2 3/8" x 10"
(4) 2 3/8" x 5 3/4"

Use an accurate 1/4" seam allowance and 15 stitches per inch.

Making the Points of the Leaves

Use the 2 3/4" x 5 1/2" pieces for the leaves and the 2 3/4" x 22" strip of the light background.

1. Draw on 2 3/4" square lines on the wrong side of all four leaves.

2. Draw on diagonal lines.

3. Pin the four leaves right sides together to the light strip.
4. Sew on both sides of the diagonal lines.

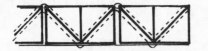

5. Cut apart on all square and diagonal lines.
6. Press the seams to the dark side.

Making the

1. Lay out one pair of each color in this order:

2. Stack them on top of each other.
3. Assembly line sew.
4. Press the seams to the dark side. Clip the threads holding them together.
5. Square them up to 2 3/8" x 4 1/8".
6. Lay out the points with the 2 3/8" x 4 1/8" pieces of each color in this order:

7. Assembly line sew them together.

Making the Stems

1. Tie a knot on the end of an 9" piece of thin cording or floss.
2. Place the cording down the center of the 1 1/2" x 4" bias strip, with the knot at the top.
3. Fold the strip in half right sides together over the cord.
4. Sew across the top and down the side. Do not catch the cord on the side.
5. Pull on the cord and turn right side out.
6. Cut the cord and repeat with the remaining three stems.

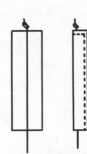

Sewing the Stems to the Light

Use the 2 3/8" x 10" light strip and the 2 3/8" squares of each color.
1. Lay the light strip on the bottom.
2. Place the stem 1/4" from the top of the strip.

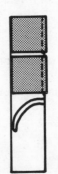

3. Place a square the same color as the stem on top. Stitch.
4. Repeat with the other stems and squares.
5. Press the seam to the dark side.
6. Cut apart.

7. Pin the stem in place 1/4" from the end.

8. Blind hem stitch with invisible thread.

Sewing the Stems and the Points

1. Lay the two pieces out in this order:

2. Assembly line sew.
3. Clip the threads holding them together.

4. Stack up the remaining points of the
   leaves and the 2 3/8" x 10" strip in this order:

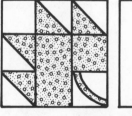

5. Flip the first point on to the strip. Stitch. Repeat with all points. Assembly line sew on the second point.

6. Cut them apart.
7. Lay them out in this order:
   Match the point carefully as you sew.

8. Square them up to 5 3/4".

Sewing the Blocks Together
1. Lay out the four leaves with the four 2 3/8" x 5 3/4"
   light pieces and the one 2 3/8" center square.
2. Sew the vertical rows.
3. Sew the horizontal rows.

Autumn Leaves is the third block in the third row.

(Optional) Machine Quilting a Three Lattice Block
1. Pin the block in the bottom center of a 16" x 19" piece
   of bonded batting.
2. "Stitch in the ditch" around each of the leaves.
3. Add a lattice strip to the left side of the block through
   all thicknesses.
4. Add cornerstones to two lattice strips. Sew them to
   the block. *See Windmill for more detail.*

Sew the Third Horizontal row together. *See Bird's Nest for more details.*

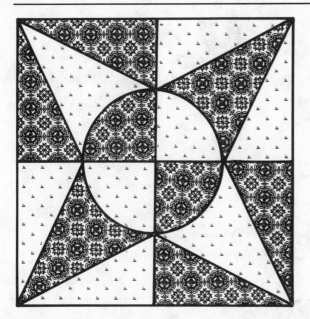

For hundreds of years after men had boats they still did not dare go far out to sea, for they had no way of telling directions when it was so cloudy! When the great age of exploring began some 500 years ago, sailors had magnetic compasses to guide them. It tells direction as the earth acts as a magnetic force pulling the compass magnet, or needle, into a north-south position. Surely Christopher Columbus had a compass deep in his pocket as he set sail to find a new route to the Far East! Quilters from around the world pay tribute to Chris for his bravery in 1492 with the October block, the Compass.

Choose a light and medium or dark.

Cutting Instructions

Layer Cut

(2) 8 1/2" x 11" pieces light   (2) 8 1/2" x 11" pieces medium or dark

Use an accurate 1/4" seam allowance and 15 stitches per inch.

Making Two   **and Two**

Piece A, the large piece in the center, is always the opposite fabric of the three smaller pieces, B, C, and D.

1. Layer the four pieces of fabric with right sides up.

2. Pin the page of templates on top of the fabric with hand sewing needles. Layer cut using the rotary cutter and ruler.

If you are short of fabric, you can individually cut each piece out of scraps.

Notice that this is a different arrangement from the way they were placed on the pattern paper. You will sew narrow ends to narrow ends.

3. Place the stacks of A, B, and C in this order:

Put the top two A pieces on the bottom of the stack so that A is a different fabric from B and C.
4. Flip B right sides together to A, matching the top edges. Assembly line sew.
5. Press the seam away from A. Snip the threads.

6. Flip AB right sides together to C. Match the top edges, and assembly line sew.

7. Press the seams away from A. Snip the threads.

8. Place D right sides together to ABC, matching up the edges.

9. Anchor the two pieces together with a few stitches. Pull A into a straight line and match D's curve as you stitch.

10. Press the seam toward D.

11. Square up each piece to 6 1/2", being careful not to trim off the seam allowances.

Sewing the Block Together

1. Lay out the pattern in this order:

2. Sew the vertical row.

3. Sew the horizontal row.

Compass is the first block in the bottom row of the quilt.

(Optional) Machine Quilting a Three Lattice Block

1. Pin the block in the bottom center of a 16" x 19" piece of bonded batting.
2. Continuously "stitch in the ditch" around the circle and each of the A pieces.
3. Add a lattice strip to the left side of the block through all thicknesses.
4. Add cornerstones to two lattice strips. Sew them to the block.

Sewing Together the Last Row in the Quilt
Compass, Turkey Tracks (November), and Snowball (December) are the three blocks in the last row. Both Compass and Turkey Tracks are Three Lattice Blocks. Notice the position of the lattice on these two blocks. Snowball is the only Four Lattice Block in the quilt.

The last row looks like this:

Compass

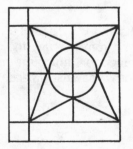

Turkey Tracks

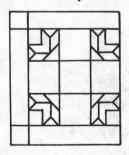

Snowball

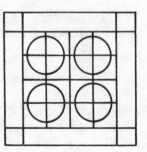

Sew this row together as you did the other three rows. *See Bird's Nest for more detail.*

30

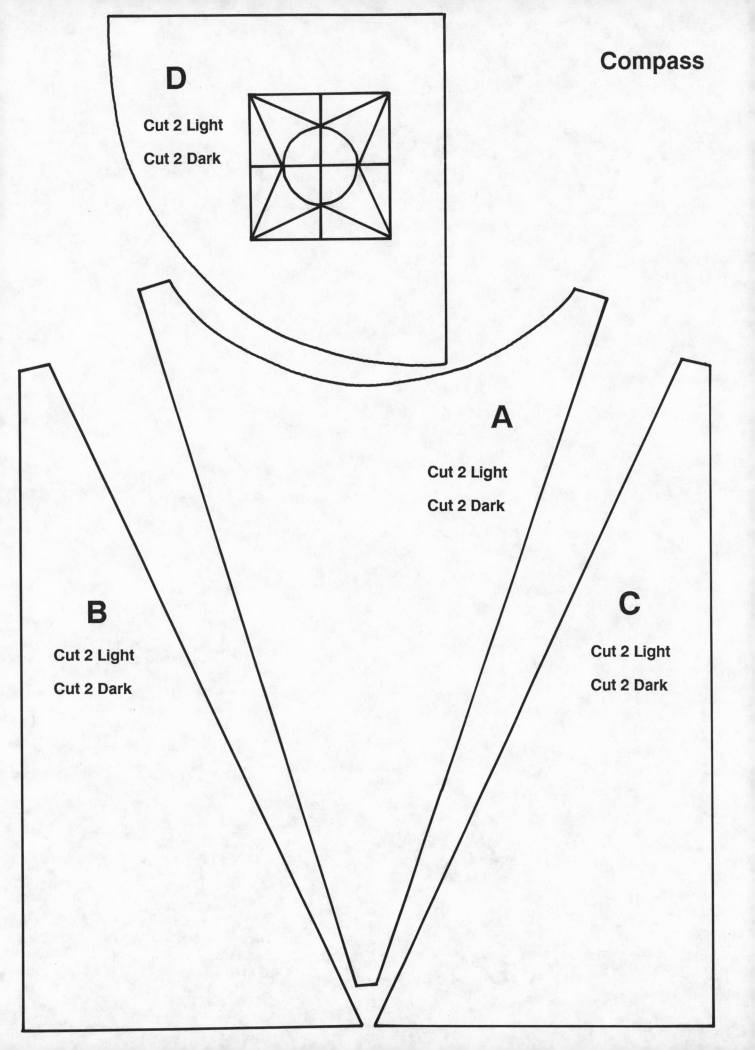

Compass

D

Cut 2 Light

Cut 2 Dark

A

Cut 2 Light

Cut 2 Dark

B

Cut 2 Light

Cut 2 Dark

C

Cut 2 Light

Cut 2 Dark

While it was the Pilgrims and Indians that memorialized the wild turkey with their first Thanksgiving celebration in the fall of 1671, Turkey Tracks was actually first known as Wandering Foot. Superstitious mothers were careful not to let their children sleep under a Wandering Foot quilt for fear they would grow up to be discontended or of a roving disposition. For the same reason, no bride would have one in her hope chest. The evil spell was broken when the name was changed to Turkey Tracks or Irish Leaf, depending on the colors used in the quilt.

Choose one light, two mediums, and two darks.

Cutting Instructions

Layer Cut

(2) 1 5/8" x 15" strips first medium
(2) 1 5/8" x 15" strips second medium
(4) 2 5/8" squares light
(2) 3 3/4" squares light

(4) 4 1/2" squares light
(2) 3" squares first dark
(1) 4 1/2" square second dark

Use an accurate 1/4" seam allowance and 15 stitches per inch.

Sewing the Feet

1. Sew the first set of medium strips with first medium on top.

2. Sew the second set of medium strips with the second medium on top.

3. Layer the strips on top of each other.

4. Lay the ruler with the 45° line across the top of the strip.

5. Cut on the 45° angle. Keeping the 45° line on the top of the strip, slide the ruler along and cut (4) 2" segments from each strip.

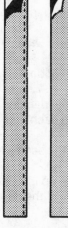

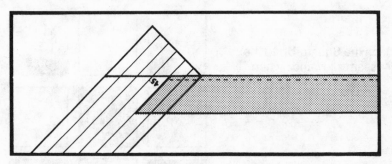

6. Open up a pair of each, and lay them out in your preferred color arrangement.

7. Press the seams of all the "toes" toward the medium color of the center two toes. Cut off the tips.

8. Lay two stacks of four each in your color arrangment.

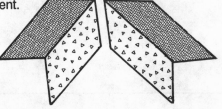

9. Assembly line sew to within 1/4" from the end of each pair. Press the seams to one side.

Inserting the 2 5/8" Squares into the Corners of the Toes

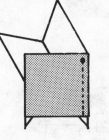
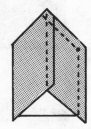

1. From the wrong side of the square, mark a dot 1/4" from one corner with a pencil.

2. Flip up the top pair of feet to expose the seam allowance 1/4" from the end.

3. Matching the pencil mark to the 1/4" mark, sew from the marks out to the outside edge of each square. Clip the threads.

4. Flip to the second side and sew from the marks out. Repeat with all squares.

Inserting the Triangles into the Toes

1. Cut (2) 3 3/4" squares in fourths on the diagonals.

Mark a dot 1/4" in on the corner on the wrong side of each triangle.

2. Fold back and gently rip out 1/4" of stitches at the points of each toe.

3. Insert the triangles as the squares were inserted.

Adding the Dark Triangles

1. Cut (2) 3" dark squares in half on the diagonals.

2. Sew the triangles to the bottoms of the toes, allowing a 1/4" tip to hang over on each end.

3. Press the seams to the dark.

4. Square up to 4 1/2", lining up the 4 1/2" mark on the Square-Up to the corners of the dark triangle. Allow for the 1/4" seam allowance when trimming.

Sewing the Block Together

1. Lay out the pieces in this order:
2. Sew the vertical rows together.
3. Sew the horizontal rows.
   Turkey Tracks is the second block in the last row in the quilt.

(Optional) Machine Quilting a Three Lattice Block
Continuously "stitch in the ditch" around the feet and center square. *See Windmill and Autumn Leaves for more detail.*

Every December the rural American woman of the 1800's was faced with the prospect of being snowbound for three months. It's easy to imagine the isolation she must have felt as she stared out her frost glazed window at the unending expanse of unbroken snowy whiteness. When she wasn't caring for her family, she had time to dream up new quilt patterns to show to her friends in the Spring. As she rearranged the shapes in Drunkard's Path, the curved pieces joined to form a circle. Understandably, with her inspiration surrounding her, she named her new block pattern Snowball. This pattern is also called Rob Peter to Pay Paul and Indiana Puzzle.

Choose a light, medium, and dark.

Cutting Instructions

Layer Cut

(8) 3 5/8" light squares
(4) 3 5/8" medium squares
(4) 3 5/8" dark squares

(8) 3 1/8" light squares
(4) 3 1/8" medium squares
(4) 3 1/8" dark squares

Use an accurate 1/4" seam allowance and 15 stitches per inch.

1. Trace the cresent square and quarter circle on template paper and cut out, or cut out the paper patterns.

2. Pin the cresent square on top of the 3 5/8" squares, cut out the curve, and discard.

3. Pin the quarter circle on top of the 3 1/8" squares, and cut around the curve.

Sewing the Pieces Together

1. Lay out the pieces in four different combinations:

Stack 4 of each.

2. With one combination, place the two shapes right sides together with the quarter circle on top.

3. Stitch 1/2" to anchor the two pieces together.

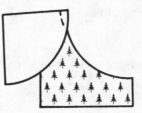

4. Equally stretch the two pieces and stitch as you stretch. Use the sewing machine needle and presser foot to anchor it as you stretch.

5. "Finger pin" the corners together. Stretch and stitch to the end.
6. Butt on the next square and continue.

7. Stretch and stitch all squares in the four combinations.

8. Press the seam toward the quarter circle.

9. Square up each piece to 3 5/8".

Sewing the Block Together

1. Lay out the block following the illustration.

2. Sew the vertical rows.

3. Sew the horizontal rows.

The Snowball block is the last block in the lower right corner of the quilt.

(Optional) Machine Quilting the Four Lattice Block

1. Pin the block to the center of the 19" square piece of bonded batting.

2. "Stitch in the ditch" around the circles.

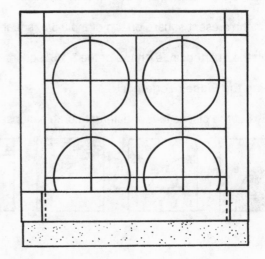

3. Add the lattice and cornerstones as on a Three Lattice Block.

4. For the last side, sew a cornerstone to each end of the lattice strip before sewing it to the block.

Sew the Fourth Horizontal Row together. *See Compass for more detail.*

Snowball

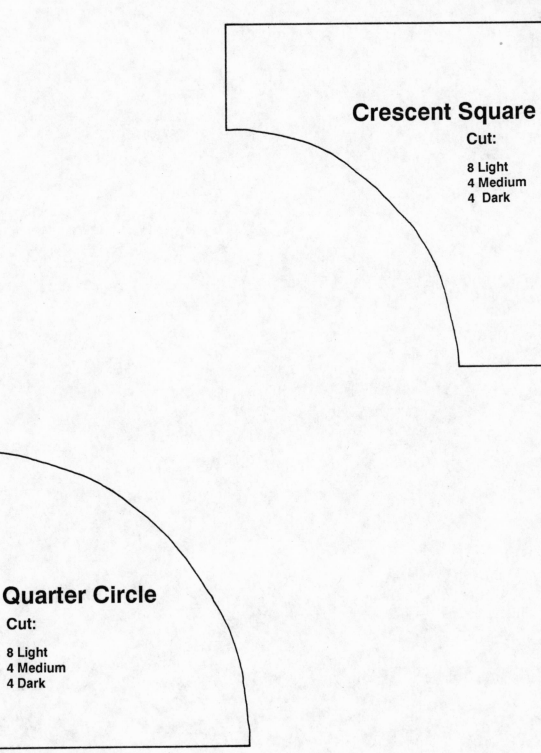

Crescent Square
Cut:

8 Light
4 Medium
4 Dark

Quarter Circle
Cut:

8 Light
4 Medium
4 Dark

(Optional) Sewing the Machine Quilted Rows Together

The four horizontal rows of blocks quilted to the batting are now sewn together into one top.

1. Place the second horizontal row right sides together to the first horizontal row. Snip the batting away from the cornerstones. Fold the batting back out of the way.

2. Match and pin the lattice and cornerstones on the two rows. Stretch or ease each lattice to fit each block as you stitch through the three thicknesses with the batting on the bottom.

3. Fold the two rows back and flat.

4. Trim away any excess batting, and hand press flat.

5. Hand whipstitch the batting flat in place.

6. Add the remaining two horizontal rows in this manner.

Refer to **"Cutting the Backing"** and **"Tying for Either a Quilted or Unquilted Top"** for remaining instruction. (Pages 39 and 40)

Sewing the Unquilted Blocks Together

Use this method of finishing your quilt if you have not machine quilted each individual block.

1. Check that each block is approximately 12 1/2" square. Square up if necessary without trimming away any part of the 1/4" seam allowance.

Do not be concerned if there is a slight variance of block sizes.

2. Lay out the finished blocks in monthly chronological order with the lattice and cornerstones.

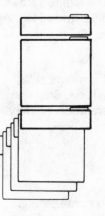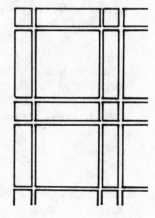

3. Flip the second vertical row right sides together to the first vertical row. Stack from bottom up with the top lattice on the top of the stack. Assembly line sew. Stretch or ease each block to fit the lattice as you stitch. Fold out.

4. Stack the third vertical row. Flip each piece right sides together to the second row as you assembly line sew. Do not cut the threads joining the pieces.

5. Repeat with all vertical rows.

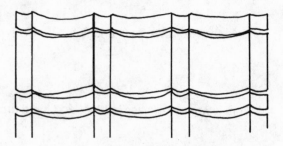

6. Lay out the quilt. Check that every block, lattice, and cornerstone is in its proper position.

7. Flip the top horizontal row right sides together to the second horizontal row. Stretch and stitch the blocks and lattice to meet as you sew.

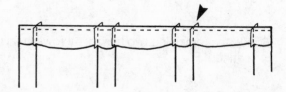

8. At the cornerstones, where the pieces are joined by threads, match the seams carefully. Push one seam up on one side and one down on the other side.

9. Continue sewing all horizontal rows.

Cutting the Backing for Either a Quilted or Unquilted Top

1. Cut into two equal pieces and remove the selvages.

2. Seam together the edges that were originally the selvages. The seam will appear horizontally across the center back in the finished quilt.

3. Place the quilt right sides together to the backing.

4. Trim away the excess backing fabric.

Adding a Casing Before Sewing the Top to the Backing (Optional)

1. Cut a 3" wide strip from any leftover fabric the same measurement as the top of the quilt.

2. Turn under the two short ends 1" each. Edge stitch.

3. Place the strip right sides together to the backing 2 1/2" down from the top.

4. Stitch across the top edge of the strip. Fold the strip up and even with the top of the backing. Pin in place.

Sewing Either a Quilted or Unquilted Top to the Backing

1. Place the quilt right sides together to the backing.

2. Pin around the outside edge.

3. Stitch around the outside edge, leaving a 15" opening in the middle of one side.

4. Turn the quilted top right side out. Do not turn the unquilted top right side out.

5. Whipstitch the opening shut on the quilted top.

Quick Turning the Unquilted Top

1. Lay the bonded batting out flat. Place the quilt on top.

Trim away any excess batting.

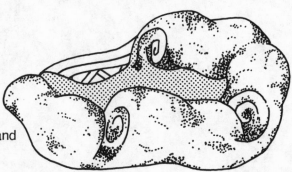

2. Station a person at each corner of the quilt. Begin rolling tightly in each corner and the sides toward the opening.

3. Open up the opening over this wad of fabric and batting, and pop the quilt right side out through the hole.

4. Unroll it right side out carefully with the layers together.

5. Working on opposite sides, grasp the edges of the quilt and pull in opposite directions to smooth out the batting.

Tying Down Either a Quilted or Unquilted Top

1. Lay the quilt out smooth on a table or large floor area.
2. Thread a curved needle with a long piece of all six strands of embroidery floss or pearl cotton for multiple tying.

3. Working from the center blocks out,
   take a stitch through all thicknesses in one
   corner of a cornerstone. Without clipping the
   threads, pull the floss to the next corner of the
   cornerstone, and take a stitch. Stitch all four
   corners with one continuous strand.

4. Clip the threads.

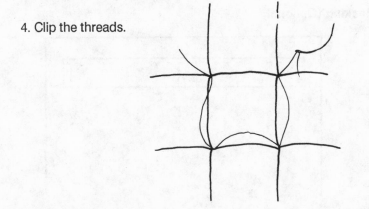
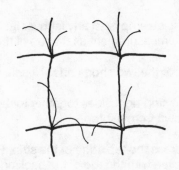

5. Take the floss on the right and wrap it
   twice around the floss on the left. Draw
   both pieces tight.

6. Take the floss on the left and wrap it twice
   around the floss on the right. Draw both
   pieces tight into a "surgeon's square knot"
   at the four corners of each cornerstone.

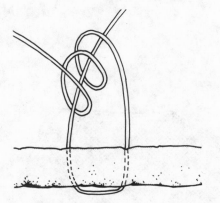
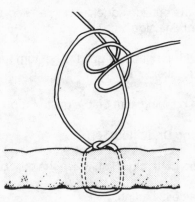

7. Clip the strands even to 1/2" length.

Order Information:

If you do not have a fine quilt shop in your area, you may write for a complete catalog and current price list of all books and patterns published by Quilt in a Day®

Books

Quilt in a Day Log Cabin
The Sampler -- A Machine Sewn Quilt
Trio of Treasured Quilts
Lover's Knot Quilt
Amish Quilt in a Day
Irish Chain in a Day
Country Christmas
Bunnies and Blossoms
May Basket Quilt
Schoolhouse Wallhanging
Diamond Log Cabin Tablecloth or Treeskirt
Morning Star Quilt
Trip Around the World Quilt
Friendship Quilt
Creating With Color
Dresden Plate Quilt, a Simplified Method
Pineapple Quilt, a Piece of Cake
Radiant Star Quilt
Blazing Star Tablecloth

Booklets and Patterns

Patchwork Santa
Last Minute Gifts
Miniature May Basket
Dresden Plate Placemats and Tea Cozy
Angel of Antiquity
Log Cabin Wreath
Log Cabin Christmas Tree
Flying Geese Quilt
Miniature May Basket Wallhanging
Tulip Table Runner and Wall Hanging
Heart's Delight, Nine-Patch Variations

Supplies Available

Rotary Cutters
Rotary Replacement Blades
Cutting Mats with Grids
6" x 6" Mini Rulers
6" x 12" Rulers
6" x 24" Rulers
12 1/2" x 12 1/2" Square Up Rulers
Cutter Kits
Magnetic Pin Cushions
Invisible Threads
Bicycle Clips
Magnetic Seam Guides
Quilting Pins
Curved Needles
Pin Basting Kits
Fairfield Batting
T-Shirts

Videos for Rent or Purchase

Log Cabin
Ohio Star
Lover's Knot
Irish Chain
Schoolhouse Wallhanging
Diamond Log Cabin
Morning Star Quilt
Trip Around the World
Flying Geese
Block Party Series One Videos
Block Party Series Two Videos
and more!

If you are ever in Southern California, San Diego County, drop by and visit the Quilt in a Day Center. Our quilt shop and classroom is located in the La Costa Meadows Business Park. Write ahead for a current class schedule and map.

Quilt in a Day®
1955 Diamond Street, San Marcos, California 92069
Order Line: 1-800- U2 KWILT(1-800-825-9458)   Information Line: 1-619-591-0081